THE *Angel* THAT WOULDN'T FALL

THE *Angel* THAT WOULDN'T FALL

SHILAYA GRANGE

XULON PRESS

Xulon Press
2301 Lucien Way #415
Maitland, FL 32751
407.339.4217
www.xulonpress.com

Printed in the United States of America.

Paperback ISBN-13: 978-1-63221-166-8
eBook ISBN-13: 978-1-6322-1167-5

Honorable mention to my friends, family, and angels that help give me strength and courage

TABLE OF CONTENTS

Prologue

AN ARMY OF ANGELS SURROUND you, working together to heal, protect, and guide you. May you find comfort in their words, faith in their protection, and love in your heart. As your days drift by and your wings become more apparent, you begin to take flight towards the sky. If your soul ever feels out of touch with the world, listen close to the whispers of your angels. Your Angels speak to you. Surrender the pain that has a hold on you, for your Angels watch from afar

Depression.

AS ONE OF YOUR ANGELS, SEE YOU stare at a blank wall trying to find answers. Answers to the pain your soul is feeling... why your heart is clenched with a grasp so tight that your breath comes out like whispers. Tears stain your cheeks and run like a shallow river... continuous... yet softly. This pain is not one that rips your heart from your chest, but one that makes your lungs constrict and your heart beat slow... down to just a whimper. Sleepless nights are no longer foreign to you. Numb is no longer the correct way to explain what your soul is feeling; and to be honest, there isn't an explanation. Your tears sting and your heart is trapped. Your soul needs hope to release it from the agony it feels. You are scared, not of the unknown, but of the simple fact that you can feel yourself slipping away into oblivion again. Depression is such a harsh word, even from the moment it touches your lips. Judgement is thrown towards you because you have pain that nobody can see. You are misunderstood, you are thought to be weak. They see you on your knees with your head down and all they see is failure. Why is that? Why do people see someone, knocked down with no strength to hold their head up properly, and instant disappointment crosses their mind? There is a reason why you drop to your knees and head down in prayer. But they don't understand that prayer is not weak... *prayer is strength.*

Pain is such a strong word; it seems in today's society, that it's something to be ashamed of. People often correlate pain with weakness, weakness not only physically, but mentally and emotionally. People gravitate to the fact that if you show your vulnerable wounds, you are beneath them...the strong person that they claim to be, and it frightens them. Why would you ever grace them with that thought of you? And so, you hide your pain. Why would you ever let yourself think of yourself or be thought of by another to be so low?

Again, I repeat…there is a reason why when you pray you climb to your knees with your head down. God knew that at your weakest point, you would need God the most. *You close your eyes because you no longer want to see; and from that moment, God is leading you.* <u>Prayer is not</u> <u>weak, prayer is strength.</u>

Mental health can be healed by spiritual belief. You are worth so much more than the words they claim you to be. You could be perfect, and they would still find a flaw in you, a reason to make you look less worthy, but you are <u>not</u>. The only person that knows the full truth of what goes on in your life is <u>you</u>. When people don't know the whole story, they tend to add and make up situations that peg judgement against you. Lashing out will cause more harm, because trying to prove their wrongful judgement of you is useless. *Wind can be silent and still move a boat, pain can still hurt but be unseen.*

I as your guardian angel am not going to tell you the right way to mend your soul, and I'm not going to tell you that you can stop it from recurring ever again. The problem is, that our soul and body will always be in battle until we get those small moments of pure God-given bliss. Those moments when your heartbeat gains speed and is full of love, you breathe clearly, and your eyes are wide open. You as a human live for those moments, the moments when your soul agrees with your body. You are not indestructible, but you are durable. Your pain may go unseen, but not unfelt. Truthfully, you are not alone because I see you. I see the way you hurt in silence; I see the way your smile desperately reaches out beyond your pain. I see the way your brave face isn't as brave as you let on. You hurt, but you have nothing to show for it. Pain within is scarier than pain brought from external sources. You are not alone, even though sometimes you may have to fight by yourself.

Anxiety.

SEE YOU AS YOU KEEP YOUR HEAD down, avoiding looking up because you do not want to see the look of defeat that reflects back at you. Your whole body shakes from the fear of what the world can do to you. It is hard to breathe because it is as if your oxygen was taken from you. You are not good enough, you are broken, weak, a disappointment in everyone's eyes. These thoughts run through your mind endlessly with nowhere to go. You feel that if you run faster and hide, the demons won't capture and consume you in the way your mind thinks. You shelter yourself and try to place a shield in front of nonexistent demons that can't even see you.

You hurt because you feel unwanted. *You are not unwanted!* Anxiety has a way of consuming you into thinking that you cannot face the world, that you cannot express yourself with confidence - *how wrong it is.* The rain pours on everyone and the wind knocks everyone from their feet. But you let the fear of failing keep you from ever giving happiness a chance.

Why do you let yourself hurt from the pain that you caused? You in your ignorance cause yourself more pain than anyone could ever bring to you. You are your biggest demon. Let your wounds bleed for everyone to see and keep the scars as reminders of what once was. Your scars bring memories of the past, but why would you focus on time that was taken from you when you are being given days ahead of you? It is possible to learn from tragedy, but not let it control the next war that you must encounter.

The battle you are facing may be silent and it may be unheard. Maybe so, but wars are made to win. No person starts a war expecting to lose. Your soul is so beautiful. You are remarkable, the elegance your soul radiates is admirable, and the strength you gain every moment that you are here on earth is one that conquers wars. You are capable of winning this war…scars and all included.

You are trembling with fear of what the world can do to you, without having the experience. How can you be frightened of an experience that you didn't even start from the beginning? Acknowledge the obstacles that bring adrenaline without fear. Jump without the fear of falling, because you know your wings will carry you before you hit the surface. If your wings ever fail you, God's arms will be the strength to catch you. Do not let the fear of the unknown create anxiety inside you. Let your faith replace your fear.

Loss.

SEE YOU, YOU FEEL EMPTINESS, COM-plete and utter hurt flows through your veins. You reach out in a panic, searching for something that isn't there any-more. You slam your eyes shut with worry and hope that your eyes deceived you into thinking that what you lost is no longer there. You ask yourself "how can something be there influ-encing my life, then it's just gone?" This is not real, this is a lie, you tell yourself that tomorrow everything will go back to exactly the way it was, but I cry along with you because trying to fool yourself and your mind is a dead-end road. You wonder why you must lose things that you love? Why does the pain and the downfall hurt so bad? Loss holds a difficult journey.

Losing something is not always a loss. Whether it is a person, something materialistic or yourself, there is always a purpose in life behind why you experienced it being taken from you. In life, everything runs off time and you and everyone feels the pressure of time on earth finally running out. Your time clock does not stop no matter how hard you try, and that includes everything living and nonliving around you. Everything and everyone runs out of time. You are put here to fulfill the time you are given and understand that your time with whatever you lost is no longer needed. The purpose and time they filled in your life is finally complete. Without things being taken from you; you cannot truly cherish the things you have. Strive to see losing something as a blessing, because without the influence it brought to your life you would not be the person you are today.

You stand blank, wrapping your arms as tight as you can to make you feel like you are here. You cry with the realization that your arms will be the support and comfort holding you up. Loss is something you as a human will never truly understand. You all work so hard for what you have and love fiercely… because if you did not, what would you have to live for?

Denial is usually the first step in loss, so you play tricks and banter with your mind trying to fool the truth. After realization, and when you become accepting, one will always ask God for one more…one more hug, kiss, touch, conversation, one more chance. The absolute cruel fact is that your wants will never be just one more. It is like asking for our favorite childhood candy once more and realizing why you fell in love with it in the first place.

Your taste becomes a craving. The sad moments will always pull harder.

Look forward with the mindset that you are better off to have had it and stare at the sky like it is the most beautiful thing that has graced your vision…because it is. See your loved one's soar and their bodies glitter because they finally got their wings. They stare back, admiring your strength, their heart looks upon you with pride because you are finally strong enough to fight the battle without them. We all want our wings, but we must

walk gracefully through the fight to get there.
Together you will be, one day, but not just yet.

LOVE AND HEARTBREAK.

I KNOW IT HURTS BECAUSE WHO CAN breathe when they no longer have oxygen? Your chest hurts, your heart is not gone, but it's completely torn apart. Why did they do this to you, why would you do this to yourself? Why are you hating yourself because you chose to love someone that did not love you? How is it possible to feel nothing and everything at the same time? They made you feel this way, they hurt you. Heartbreak is something that influences every single relationship that comes to you in the future. You are more cautious; you turn everyone down and you don't let anyone love you because you don't understand how somebody could.

Believe me when I say this, *you are loved and I need your heart to love itself.*

It is okay when you can't decide, and nothing makes sense. It is okay when you are at a point that you don't understand what you're doing or why you're here. *Please choose yourself. Be loving for yourself, be happy for yourself. Mend your soul.* Have a pure heart, because in a ruthless world that is all that truly matters.

The way an embrace can change so many outcomes, the way a kiss can make you feel things that you genuinely believed never existed, the way one single person can forever change the way your heart beats. Love is the one true, pure thing we have in this world. The passion love brings is enough to move mountains. You love so hard that you are completely convinced that this person was meant for you, looking past every sign that disagrees with you. All the love and devotion you put into someone keeps you trying to make a puzzle piece fit into a picture that is completely different. Love can carry you across mountains and sail across oceans. Your heart was not taken from you, it has just been broken. Everything that has been broken can be put back together. I need you to listen to me when I say *someone needs your love.* Just because something fell apart does not mean that you cannot recreate it. Rise up and wear your heart on your sleeve. You shouldn't care if it's bruised and beaten, because no powerful warrior has come out of a fight unscarred. Be a warrior, show your scars, let people see the fight you have been through, so you can stand proud and say that you have won.

Your heart does not give up on you. Your heart pumps and gives you life, holding you together even when it feels completely torn apart. *Isn't it lovely, how much your own heart loves you. Why would you ever refuse love to something that has never, not even once, stopped loving you? If you cannot love anyone or nothing in this world, at least choose to love your own heart. Choose the love that will never stop loving you.*

Your Purpose.

SEE YOU STRUGGLING WITH QUES-
tions. Why am I here? Why am I stuck
in a world that has no idea who I am.
These thoughts scream inside your head unan-
swered. You walk the streets and can't help
but wonder the reasoning behind your existence. You no longer cry when you see pain,
you cry when you see happiness. The pain you
feel is numb without a sting. You avoid happiness like it's a bad sickness, yet you welcome
sadness with open arms. The human being
will always ask why, why am I experiencing
the trials and tribulations that I am? What is
my purpose?

You open your eyes in the morning to an
emptiness with no answers to your being.
People tell you to be happy, to live in the

precious moments you are given and expect you to mend perfectly to the life you live. But what is a life worth living without purpose? Why be here on earth, blankly walking through a world that cannot even see you. You put your faith in a higher being, hoping it will bring answers. You can only hope for so long before you let go of any need you have behind your purpose.

Your eyes wander around to see happiness, you see the living that seem to have a clear path to their reasoning and instantly your heart clenches. Mine tightens for yours as I see the pain on your face. You always look with wonder and envy of why your answers cannot be so clear. *Life blurs your vision when you are unable to follow the path you are given.* Have you ever wondered when you have happy moments why you can see so clearly; you can see every detail creating a perfect picture of you in that moment. The world wants to remind you that it is not so bad, that you have reasoning to be here breathing. You have a purpose to the path you walk down.

Some will walk their path with blind eyes in hopes that it will prevent them from ever wondering the purpose behind their existence. Some walk their path noticing every detail, every reason behind the life they live. Be the second person. Acknowledge every detail of your life and understand that without it you would not have made it to the destination you are at now. Life has many shortcuts, but most come with a scene that is not a shortcut and seems less lovely. Walk with certainty that the path you are on is the right one. You do not need shortcuts to make it to the finish line. Like every race, there is an end goal... an ending. The ending is inevitable so why are you in such a hurry, instead of admiring the simple fact that it is not over? Life is not a race of who is the fastest, but one you have to stop and admire on the way.

Every laugh, smile, embrace, and word has purpose. These have a purpose not only to your life, but to every single existence around you. *Whichever path your feet may wander down, God's hand will be in yours and your wings will follow.*

Admitting Defeat.

I SEE YOU RUNNING, FIGHTING, AND reaching for something that cannot be obtained. You try and try again to finish the race but fall short every time. You will never understand why you can't just win. Why can't you have what you want? You won't say it, you won't tell the world that you have failed. My beautiful light, the world sees you. We all see you fall, but you refuse to let the world see you give up. By refusing to let the world see your pain and see your downfall, you cause the most brutal war on yourself. Why would you run a race and pack more weight on your shoulders with every step? It is okay to fail, especially when you're running a race that continues in a never-ending cycle.

Why are you so scared to admit that you have failed? Are you scared of the judgment, the pitiful looks? The world has already seen the damage and they continue to go through the daily motions of life. The first step in healing your wounds, your wings, your dignity, is admitting that you have failed, because the only person you are going to hurt is yourself. Stop trying to fool your own mind, stop telling yourself that you can withstand continuous punches to your life and not feel the pain. Hurting is part of the human experience.

The reflection staring back at you looks beaten, broken, tired, you look defeated. One thing I learned is our body gives up long before our souls ever will. Your soul holds onto any possible meaning to life in attempts to not let you fall. Tell your soul it is okay to let go, give it reassurance that you will be on your knees right next to it. Let the whole world see you fall to your knees.

I am sure your life has been a wave of downhill spirals lately and at one point you almost gave up. Sometimes when the weight of the world is on your shoulders, you feel the need to drop to your knees. One thing you should learn is to never feel ashamed of dropping to your knees when times get rough. Yes, outsiders may look at you like your weak, a mess, or maybe that you gave up, but the moment you hit your knees is the moment God can help you. When you pray and you put your trust in the fact that everything God is putting you through is a path to your ideal life, that is when everything that put you there will no longer matter. The best thing you can do for yourself is trust in God and your plan, even when you can no longer trust anyone or anything else. Life is hard, you are going to cry and hurt and make bad decisions; but all that should matter to you is the fact God kept you here on Earth for another day. God sees that your journey is not over and sits and watches you discover it. The only person that should ever believe in yourself more than God, is you. *Find your passion and live for it. Love everyone even when you do not get it in return. But most importantly do not give up on yourself, because the good Lord upstairs never has.*

THE VIEW OF
BEING PERFECT.

WANT YOU TO KNOW THAT IT IS A battle that can never be won, something you strive for but can never conquer. You tell yourself that anything less than perfect is unacceptable. Humans do not entirely understand how wrong that mindset is. When somebody wants to be perfect and without flaw, it usually correlates with how others will think of them. Why would you ever spend your whole life trying to convince yourself and others that you are a completely different person than the person God has created you to be? Mistakes are something every life form indulges in; because without them, we would have no idea of the right thing to do.

Why do you try to take a beautiful canvas, created by the world's artists, and just throw paint on it in hopes that it will cover up the true picture underneath? You are a canvas, a beautiful piece of art, and you have the ability to show the world just how vibrant and enticing you can be. If your wings will carry you throughout this life, why are you clipping them and preventing yourself to fly above what other minds speak? Perfect should be kept in your oblivious state of mind, perfect is a word that brings more hate in this world than it will ever bring love. Replace the word perfect with *unique* and watch your outlook on yourself completely change. *You are uniquely beautiful, incredible, magnificent. You are a work of art, a free-hand sketch that was painted with vibrant colors. Your soul shines through, adding the finishing touches to the piece of fine art that you are.*

Do not let the naysayers convince you that your art doesn't belong in the gallery we call the world. You are *unique,* you will be treasured by the highest bidders the moment you start believing you belong here. You do belong here; the world needs you here.

Like any beautiful creation, you will be viewed differently by each eye. Just because people have different views on the way they see the external you, does not mean they have, or will ever get the chance, to see the real you. Every piece of art ever created has masked beauty, that only if you look deeply enough will you truly see. The problem with hidden beauty is that it cannot be seen through one's eyes, but only with one's hearts. You choose who sees what lies beneath the external facade that you show to the world. Not everyone deserves to experience your hidden gems, everyone does not deserve to see the real you. Put your mind at ease by knowing that you have so many hidden talents about you that are only shared if you let them. If you choose not to show your vulnerable side, that does not make you any less worthy than they are. Perfect is not what you are, but who you are. *You are indescribably unique with so much goodness in your heart. A beautiful canvas waiting for the next picture to be created.*

SINNERS
DISCRETION.

WANT TO TALK TO YOU ABOUT THIS concept. You perceive that your sins or negative experiences are something that will always be capable of holding you back. When you progress in life you will always wonder why on earth you let yourself indulge in something that would impact your life and your mind in a hurtful way. Those are the demons doing the Devil's work. Humans always try to erase their negative decisions, in hopes they will dissipate into oblivion. Whether you sin daily, or it comes in waves, the only thing you must understand is that you are not alone. Sins can be forgiven, sometimes forgotten, but never without consequence. The consequences of your actions are not always the prettiest picture, but they are deemed necessary.

A perfect world without sin sounds reassuring, without trial, and intriguing. Just like sins, too much of something causes complete destruction. There needs to be bad choices in life in order to live. Your brain needs to experience everything, the good and the bad, so you can understand your choices and then categorize them. Just because you view others coping mechanisms as wrong, you have no right to tell them so. They are indulging in that sin to decide within themselves what is right from wrong. Sins cannot tell us who we are, but they do make us into who we want to be.

Do you know what it feels like to slowly fall apart inside? My condolences go out to my own heart and your' s if pain is ever inflicted upon its tender nature. You cry for your own heart and your sanity; but nevertheless, you do not show pain. You keep pushing through every waking moment with merely the thought that God has a plan for you. You have gotten close to giving up, you have been right on the brink of letting everything go. But your faith inside is too strong to ever give your life away and waste everything that the yesterday's you have worked for. Do not blame anyone for this pain, not even yourself. Blaming others on the mishaps of your tragedies and holding grudges does nothing but inflict pain on yourself. People in today's society feed off the pain of others, they strive to be above everyone and everything. They think that their own selfishness puts them above God. The moment you let your behavior put you in the position that you no longer trust in God, and you believe you are above God's plan for you, is the moment you run helplessly through a world that wants nothing more than to hold you in place.

The demons of the world feed off lost souls. The only being that can guide you through the pain and tragedy of this world, the only one that can protect you from your own selfishness, is God. The moment God stretches his hand out to you for you to take it and follow, is the moment you step up to your fate. God does not judge, does not inflict pain on the innocent, and does not sit and wait for you to believe in the path for you. The decision is yours whether you want a map to follow and a trusted hand, or to run endlessly in a box with no corners. You are not wrong for taking the journey less travelled. *God does not judge or hate the ones that choose the second journey for themselves, God merely puts hope in them. The last thing I will say to you is, sometimes angels fall too.*

TIDES IN MY SOUL.

FOR JUST A SECOND, LOOK WITH ME to see your external being and your soul as two different lifeforms. Your soul can live on without you, but your body cannot live without your soul. Although your soul does not need to, it still chooses you. Your soul did not only choose to live for you, but it chose to die with you. Isn't it completely humbling to know that it gifted all of itself for a chance you could live and journey through life? The moment you come into this world you are no longer separate beings, but you have become one together. Your souls' choice is not a temporary pass of time, but a promise to never leave you. If you choose to leave, your soul will leave with you. Together you are one.

You feel everything, heartbreak, pain, happiness, even love.

As a human, your first reaction to trauma and pain is to create a strong force field inside you, completely drowning your soul in your sorrows. Your eyes fill with oceans refusing to fall and replenish your gasping spirit. Eventually, your tears will overflow and pour out into the world. How can you ever see the beautiful light your soul radiates without draining your body of your pain? There is a reason rainbows come after thunderstorms. Let all the grief and pain become something wonderfully magnificent. Let your soul shine.

Why do we bottle up our tears and create a hurricane inside us that is just waiting to destroy every part of our being when we are completely in control of the storms? Let your tears stain your cheeks and create rivers that flow through your body to your heart. Let the river run through you, let the tears fall and feed the earth of your sorrows. Become a powerful waterfall instead of a lonely shoreline. Do not lose your soul in the depths of your despair at your own conceit.

Pain must be felt, but it also must be let go. Your soul will hold you together and keep you afloat through the worst of times. Be the legs that move, the voice that takes pride, and continues to give your soul hope and love through every single trial that you will encounter in life together.

Provide hope in your words to give reassurance that your faith in each other is strong as one. Stronger than any hurricane, thunderstorm, or tragedy. *Do not lose your soul, because you will also lose yourself.*

BAD CIGARETTES.

*F*OR ONCE IN YOUR LIFE YOU GAIN clarity, finally seeing the strong grasp others have on your emotions. They use your weaknesses against you in a form of addiction. Without using pain to enforce the role they play in your life, they feel withdrawn. Narcissistic people will always hold your mental faults against you to provide satisfaction within themselves. Weakness in others brings a form of stimulation to the mind, they want to see you fall so they can rise. They control you without hesitation, they feed off your emotions unapologetically. Do you want to live your whole life letting others control you? You live in the mockery they create; you have fallen vulnerably right into their hands.

The truth in the matter is that they are frightened of you, they see how much power and greatness you have and want to destroy it before it is seen in the light. The thing about people that need control, is that they become obsessed with how your brain thinks, in hopes they have a hold on your mind. But instead, they start to become you as if they are your shadow. They steal your thoughts, your words, your existence. They become addicted to you, constantly checking up on your life in hopes their plan has not faltered. They will not let you take their addiction away from them.

Once you try to take yourself away from an addict, they become frantic. You are all their mind can see, completely clouding their vision to the great measures they have gone to get what they want. Just like a bad cigarette you place yourself right into their hands because you do not know how to tell them to quit.

With every single word you take in, it creates a blackness inside of you, the words slowly killing you. You do not even realize that you are the spark of fire that lights their bad habits. They are completely satisfied with you, entirely enthralled with your existence. You have no more fight in you, the darkness is taking you with it because you no longer try to pull away. The demons are dragging you down further and further, they rip and tug trying to free your hand of the hold on the rope that claims your sanity. The darkness knows that it does not always just take one hard pull, but if they continue to tear you down, your hand will eventually let go.

Choose to fight, and by fight I don't mean retaliate. People take the word fight in the form of a war and that they must destroy the threat. When you hear the words "you *need to fight* " the first thing you should do is *not let go* . Protect yourself but do not feed gasoline to a burning fire. We all want peace, but most will not contribute to the effort.

There will always be a shadow following you into the light in hopes that the light will reach their face instead of yours. They follow your path instead because they are too frightened to follow their own. There is a reason your shadows are behind you, some with good intentions but most with poor energy towards you. In the world it is hard to decipher who has you in their best interest, but God gives you the choice to decide that on your own. God gives you the choice of who is seen in your light and who can lurk in your shadows. Follow the light with open eyes and a willing heart and the dark souls that are behind you will render in the black abyss that follows you everywhere. Worship is your weapon.

The light that comes from your soul attracts the energy it puts off into the world. Let your heart be the reflection that shines through and allows your soul to follow effortlessly. You can acknowledge that there is darkness yet keep it blind to your vision. You cannot be frightened of something that you pay no mind to. *You are the light that keeps the darkness in the shadows.*

MIRRORS.

SEE YOU AS YOU STAND NAKED, VUL-nerable in front of your biggest critic. You search for something that looks alive. You try to find just one thing that you love about yourself but come up empty handed. This is too big, too small, not straight enough, I'm not beautiful, why was I given these scars? When you see yourself, all you can do is look with disgust and envy of who you wish you could be. You twist and turn in front of the mirror searching for something you could love, but the reflection that looks back at you is one that is completely broken. I see how hurt you are and the tears that fall down your face, oh how I wish I could wipe them away. You are walking through a life with no destination, oh how I wish I could take your hand and lead you. Your silent sobs in the night that go unheard, oh how I wish I could tell you I was listening. The thoughts running through your mind telling you to give up and let go, oh how I wish I could tell you that you are almost there. I look in every reflection praying you find comfort in the fact that God has a plan for you. You take endless stabs at your back, and your heart yet still refusing to fall, oh how I wish I could tell you to drop to your knees and pray. Whispers into the world have the power to be heard, God is listening. Your physical beauty does not define your worth. You may not think you are perfect or that you could ever be wanted, but that is the biggest lie that has ever left your lips. We all lie to ourselves every single day making ourselves seem like less than we are. How are you supposed to love others when you do not even love yourself?

What are your excuses for not loving every single part of your being, even the messy parts? You are God's creation, a complete masterpiece, believe that you deserve yourself. You avoid looking around because all you see is your reflection staring back at you. Could you imagine a world with no mirrors? Never once being able to see what you truly look like on the outside and strictly going off others' opinions of you. Always being vulnerable and having to trust that people think you are beautiful because you could never say otherwise.

Your scars, face, eyes, and your appearance tell the story of who you are. When you look in the mirror you need to decide who you are and learn that it is extraordinary to be different. There is only one person in the world that can be you. It breaks my heart that you can look at the sky, the mountains, and nature and think it is breathtaking, as if God didn't also create you. Every existence was handcrafted, made to be different and unique. *God took time on the stars but outdid himself with you. Do not let your fear destroy who you are.* You don't have to live your life trying to impress the world. Imagine how much love and devotion you put into other people that you take away from yourself. *The first step in healing is learning to forgive.* Forgive yourself for ever thinking such harsh things about yourself. Listen to your love and whisper your prayers. The biggest cries out to God are sometimes spoken in a voice from within. Choose to view yourself with the same standards as you see the beauty of the world.

You are capable of climbing the highest mountains and swimming the harshest of seas. If you are capable of such great things, then I truly believe you are capable of falling in love with every inch of your being. The stars speckle the sky with blemishes of light, and we view them as beautiful. *The stars tell stories of millions of galaxies and planets just like your scars tell the stories of who you are. Let your scars represent your story.*

No matter who you are, someone needs what you have, and you are destined to bring it to them. You owe it to yourself to be proud of who you are. You owe it to the world to give the gift that God gave you. *God placed a special gift in every single existence he has created. Someone or something's life would be lacking without you in it. You are loved, you are wanted, you are needed.*

Isn't it Beautiful?

ISN'T IT BEAUTIFUL THE WAY THE SUN kisses the sky every morning and the moon tells the world goodbye at sunrise? The stars shine alongside the moon giving it reassurance that it is not alone in the darkness. The ocean crumbles mountains and the ground holds your feet up. The sun, moon, and stars have never left you. Isn't it also beautiful that your lungs breathe and your heart pumps? That your eyes see, and your ears listen. You are blessed with beauty and gifts to truly experience life. Look at the moon with comfort knowing that although it said goodbye it will be back again tomorrow. And see the sun watching you with love and admiration. Know that although the sun shines brighter, the stars still shine. The stars shine for the moon in a world full of black. And the sun shines for you.

God gives you wings to fly and kiss the sky, but just like the stars and moon you have a promise to your existence. The sun wakes you up in the morning and shines for you, the moon brings calmness and comfort for you to rest. The stars give you light so you do not feel completely alone, and the oceans carry you places that land never could. Mountains give you existence on earth and a place to roam. In light, we see the essence of color and the places we are meant to go.

In the darkness, we are able to truly admire a world that is beautiful without color.

You see an extraordinary world, but you don't see you. You do not see the way your face lights up and brings color to the ones surrounding you. You do not see the peaceful slumber as you rest which brings comfort to the one that lays next to you. You don't see the way you move people with your words or actions, and you don't see the way you lift people back up to their feet by giving them a shoulder to cry on. *But, my dear one, I see you.*

So, isn't it beautiful, the things you do? The way you heal and change so many other lives around you. You may be small in size, but the impact you have on the world is greater than you realize, bigger than mountains, oceans, stars, the moon and even the sun.

CPSIA information can be obtained
at www.ICGtesting.com
Printed in the USA
LVHW070405061020
668044LV00020B/255

9 781632 211668